Being Autistic

C000146556

Nine adults share their journeys from discovery to acceptance

Edited by Caroline Hearst

www.autangel.org.uk

Copyright 2015–2019 AutAngel CIC.
Copyright of the content of individual contributions remains with the named author.

ISBN 978-1-78280-489-5

Introduction Caroline Hearst

❝A starting point for your exploration❞

This book was conceived by autistic adults. We wished such stories had been available for us when the shock of recognition, and the personal understanding we gained from our awareness of ourselves as autistic people, subsided and left us wondering 'where to from here?'

We were looking for something to help us grow as autistic adults and give us a sense of community; we hope this book will do that for you. It includes contributions from autistic people whose stories offer an opportunity to witness how the journey – towards being in the world as a self-aware autistic individual – has been navigated by others. As you explore this territory you might find that both the terrain itself and your view of it change and evolve. Many of us feel immense relief and elation on finding that there is explanation and a name for the difference we have felt, tried to disguise, but been unable to describe, all our lives. Others are deeply affected by the stigma that still attaches to autism and deny that the diagnosis could apply to them.

'When I first learned about autism, I wanted nothing to do with it. Then, that led to me, reluctantly accepting it just wasn't going anywhere, and I called myself a person with autism. Now, though, I think of myself as an autistic person, with a family of other autistic people (even if we are far apart).

'Autscape[1] has meant I see my differences as part of the differences that make up the whole of humanity and as something to be celebrated, not something I need to get away from,' is how Amanda describes this shift in Asperger United.[2]

Even when being identified as autistic is initially experienced as positive, there can be sadness when realising that while everything may have changed in our inner world, in the outer world everything is still the same. It can be hard to know where to take our new found identity, how to take it there and whom to share it with. These are not simple matters; if we want our external world – our lives – to change as much as our internal world we might need, in Gandhi's words, to 'be the change'.

Fortunately, we do not have to travel alone. Recently many autistic communities have developed and flourished. There are websites, forums and organisations where you can connect with other autistic people. This can be very helpful and affirming, it can also be confusing and disappointing. Autistic people have many and varied talents as well as challenges; autistic groups and communities reflect that diversity, both internally in the membership of the group and structurally, in the way the group operates.

I hope that these stories will offer a starting point for your exploration and that some will resonate with you and help you on your journey. Bon Voyage.

---

1 Autscape is an annual conference/retreat run by and for autistic people.
2 September 2013. Asperger United is published by the National Autistic Society.

I'm OK   Liane Collins

"I had decided that it didn't suddenly disable me – I was still the same person"

My son was diagnosed with autism when he was three years old. I was devastated. I had absolutely no idea what it was. However, his diagnosis led me down the path of university and a completely new career. I hated my job as a midwife anyway. I never managed to do it well or get on with anyone and I didn't know why. I did a degree in psychology, another in science and a post grad certificate to teach. I got on well with the children – less so with the other teachers. But it put me in a good position to see my son got the best education we could manage in our area. He is now 24.

As I taught others, and lived with my son, and learned more about autism I was certain it was genetic and had come from my husband. With his engineering and scientifically minded brain and slight 'oddities' it seemed obvious. I never considered that it could be me. After all, it was rare in girls (wasn't it?!) and I didn't really fit the same patterns. Besides, I'd left teaching and added to the collection of letters after my name with counselling and was working in a career where empathy was very necessary – and I knew I had a high degree of that – maybe even a bit more than I would have liked.

I specialise in working with people with Asperger's Syndrome and I work mostly online. I have a few reasons for doing so, but to be truthful it also suits me better than face to face work. Far less exhausting! By now you may be seeing what I had missed.

I was working with a lady who self-diagnosed as Asperger's, very high functioning, and I identified with her very strongly – much more so than I usually would with a client. She told me about a book by Rudy Simone she had read, and in light of work research I also bought it and read it. It was a stereo-typical light bulb moment – I was reading about myself.

I spent the next year researching autism in girls, reading everything I could get my hands on. I joined groups and spoke to other women who identified as having autism. I started a journal, considering the things I was reading and being told and applying them to memories I had of my own experiences of growing up and coping with life. When I was completely convinced I went to speak to my GP. It didn't take much to convince her and I was referred for diagnosis. I was horrified to find I was on a two year waiting list! There was nothing I could do about that though so just carried on with life, biding my time and learning more as I went on. After 18 months I received a letter to say the NHS diagnosis service had closed and there were no plans to reinstate a psychologist to carry on. The waiting list was handed (with dubious confidentiality issues) to the local city council to send on to other agencies who may be able to arrange support. Fortunately during this time I had met a social worker who had trained in diagnosis and was one of those the list had been allocated to. She added me to her list.

The assessment procedure was done in a place I didn't know and I had no idea what was going on. I was very much out of my comfort zone – and that of course was the point. I was already convinced that I had Asperger's and so the diagnosis, when it finally came, was no real surprise – though it was very strange, and quite an emotional experience to see it written down for the first time. There were many things picked up by being filmed that I hadn't been aware of and many others that I recognised as learned responses from my years of teaching and counselling and trying to be 'normal'.

So, how has realisation/diagnosis affected me? From the first I had decided that it didn't suddenly disable me – I was still the same person I had always been. I just had a bit more understanding about where I was coming from as a person. The long wait for diagnosis had given both my husband and myself time to learn more about it and come to terms with it.

He recognised that I didn't change as a result of diagnosis; he just noticed things about me more. I had also decided that it was a reason for the way I thought and did things, but it was certainly not an excuse.

I am able to acknowledge some of the issues of my clients – but they are not I, and I am not they. We are all different; we perceive and experience the world in different ways – as with any other client. It gives me some credibility when I am asked for information from peers and in my writing. I am part of a special group.

I also see this, as written by Dr. Ruth Baker,[1] as a signpost and not a label. It indicates to me now where I have been and also gives me some direction to where I am going. It has made me much more self aware and less concerned about just being me. Yes I'm immature, naïve and gullible. I am obsessive, compulsive and need collections. I am happy on my own and would rather spend special birthdays and anniversaries with a pizza and a film with my husband and son (and cat). I live in books – they are my sanctuary. I am a little odd and my husband occasionally gazes at me in disbelief. I am me – and that is ok. I am ok.

---

1 'Diagnoses are often thought of as labels but they could also be considered as signposts. Signposts do something more than labels they help people find their way on a journey'.

Cat lady finds her way Laura Williams

> **"All those times I thought I was unlikeable – it turns out I am actually quite a nice person really"**

If I asked you to go up to a Japanese person and start up a conversation in Japanese, you would argue, 'but I don't speak Japanese!' You might ask me whether I knew any Japanese words. Imagine how frustrated you would feel if I refused to tell you any Japanese, and still expected you to go and speak Japanese. Would you feel nervous in this situation? What would give you the self-confidence to feel comfortable with talking Japanese? Therapy to try and persuade you that you really could speak Japanese? Or how about if I sat down with you for five minutes and taught you a few Japanese words?

Well I am afraid I would not really be able to help you much in this situation as I do not actually speak any Japanese. Nor do I really speak much Human. I went through my whole childhood knowing that I was very different to other children, not being able to understand them, and finding friendships very difficult to form, and to maintain. I knew it could not be everyone else's fault, as they were not bad people. I just did not know how to get people to like me. I knew the issue lay with me. I knew I was not a bad person, but I knew there was something about me that prevented people from liking me.

Whenever I asked for help I was reassured there was nothing wrong with me and I should have more self-confidence. I found this extremely frustrating, as the reason I was scared to talk to people was not because I lacked self-confidence, it was because I did not know what on earth to say! The more I asked for help, the more I was told I had social anxiety, and just needed to talk to people anyway. Everyone ignored what I was saying when I told them I still did not know what to say, and persisted that I did really, but was just too anxious to say it.

When I was about 21, a colleague told me about his son who had Asperger's. He suggested I might have it too. I started reading about Asperger's on the internet and thought a lot of it did sound like me. I started to think I might have finally found an explanation for my difficulties.

But then I read that Asperger's was a type of autism and thought, 'oh no, I don't have a learning disability, I am intelligent, I have A Levels,' and forgot about the idea.

It was a couple of years later that I read a newspaper article written by a woman with Asperger's. I wish I could remember who! The article was about how she felt, rather than the clinical information I had been reading about how people with Asperger's appear to others. I related to it so strongly that I had to start looking up Asperger's again.

I joined an internet forum and communicated with other adults with Asperger's, and found I had a lot of difficulties and concerns in common with them. But I still felt that many aspects of Asperger's did not relate to me. Eventually I plucked up the courage to speak to my husband about it. He pointed out many things that I was unaware of. I now realise that is part of the condition – that I am often unaware of how I appear to others because it is difficult for me to see things from another person's point of view.

I started to try out hints and tips shared by other people from the internet forum. I learned that first impressions are really important, and that you can get away with making mistakes later if you have already given a good first impression. I had found it hard to make friends at work, and wondered what I was doing wrong when I saw people chatting to each other, and wished I could have friendships like that too. So I started making a big effort to remember to smile and say hello when I passed a colleague in the corridor. The difference was amazing. All of a sudden people started actually talking to me, asking how my weekend was. Because I finally spoke to them, they realised what I was hiding inside: that I am actually quite nice really.

I still could not make that step from friendly acquaintances to friendship, but at least it was a start. It was the start of being more comfortable around work colleagues, but it was the start of something far more important as well. I realised that although I was never going to be normal, understanding what the problem actually was meant I could make changes to create a much happier life.

I was diagnosed with Asperger's Syndrome in 2007 at the age of 25. I was so relieved to have an explanation for all the difficulties I had experienced through school and my early adult life, and which still persisted. It helped me feel comfortable trying out more and more of the techniques I'd read about.

All those times I thought I was unlikeable – it turns out I am actually quite a nice person really; it's just that I often give people the wrong impression. When I meet a new person I would like to be friends. I show this by saying nothing, and failing to make eye contact or smile at them. After a while I feel so awkward that I make some excuse and go away. It is understandable really that they get the wrong impression!

I'm learning. Gradually noticing the things I'm getting 'wrong' that give people the wrong impression of me, and working out ways to give out the right impression instead. It's not about changing my personality (there is nothing wrong with my personality); it's about working out how to communicate myself in ways that people understand.

I have a lot of difficulties with executive function which mean I cannot manage the things I want to do. These difficulties do not go away when I am with other autistic people, and would still prevent me living life to the full even if I lived in some parallel autistic universe. For this reason, I see my autism as more than just a difference; I see it as a disability.

But accepting that I have a difficulty in this area has enabled me to discover and use strategies designed to help. I have lists, alarms, reminders, calendars, prompts, charts everywhere. They don't resolve the problem, but they help immensely. Now I remember better to take medication, eat meals, go to bed, choose sensible clothes, get to work (roughly) on time, watch TV programmes, find time for my hobbies. All these things help me live more independently and enjoy life, which are important to me.

Before I was diagnosed I just tried harder and harder to remember things, but still forgot, and thought I must be stupid. Accepting I have a disability and implementing appropriate strategies makes me more able than I was before.

Learning new skills to negotiate situations helped me feel better about myself. I realised that although some things are hard, I can still achieve a lot. I have learned new social skills and now I feel like I can cope with social situations I previously would have avoided, because not knowing how to handle them made them just too scary. Aged 30 I finally felt ready to go to university, and now I am about to start my third year. I am getting acceptable grades, my degree should lead to the kind of work I will love, and I have made some lovely friends. Without the diagnosis and the positive changes it has enabled me to make to my life, I never would have considered university.

I married at the age of 23. My husband loved to socialise, and he helped to facilitate conversations and when we went out together, and I was able to meet new people and make some friends. When he was not with me though, I still didn't have the skills to negotiate the social world. I only felt comfortable when he was by my side. We did not know about autism when we met, and we both thought my problem was simply shyness and he did everything he could to help. And this he did to the best of his abilities.

However, my husband wanted to help me get 'better' and become normal. Our relationship was already faltering due to many reasons, but the realisation that I had autism, a lifelong

condition, was the final straw in our marriage. The diagnosis was confirmed just a month before our divorce was finalised, and the adventure I have been on since then is one I have had to undertake alone.

A diagnosis of autism does change the way other people can view you, even those closest to you. But it can also change the way you view yourself, give you a starting point to work out how to make things better, and build a positive future for yourself.

Validated Alison

"For me, a diagnosis meant validation"

It's a frightening world when you feel different. You don't know why, but you know that everything feels difficult and you persistently come up against problems, but you tell yourself that it must be like that for everyone. But deep down you feel really unlucky. Is it really this difficult for everyone? Were you born with a black cloud over your head! And then, sometimes fortuitously, for instance when you are researching reasons for your child's extreme behaviour, you come up against the word "Asperger's", and suddenly you have an epiphany. There are others like you, you aren't defective or wrong, it's not your fault. You're just different. That's you.

I first found out about Asperger's (which I'd never previously heard of) six years before I was finally diagnosed.

For me, a diagnosis meant validation. Because even though I knew I had it once I'd read about it, I could just be kidding myself right? I could just be latching onto something which seemed to fit, to wrap everything up neatly into a box and maybe I was really just a mixed-up, difficult person after all and maybe life is meant to be this difficult. All the research I have done since finding out about Asperger's, has only further cemented my understanding and acceptance of my diagnosis and of what it means for me as a person. It helps me understand why I have the difficulties I do (*sensory*, *overload, shut down, executive dysfunction and more).* Having a professional write a report to say it in black and white, made all the difference.

For me, (as with many Aspies[1]), honesty and being believed are vital, and had I not received a diagnosis I would have been made to feel like a fraud even though I knew I had Asperger's. That would have been an invalidation of my very being. Of course, once you have the diagnosis it's not necessarily plain sailing either, because receiving the support you may need depends very much on where you live and how much your local authority and NHS departments adhere to the Autism Strategy[2]! It hasn't been professionals who have helped me learn about my condition, it has been my own research and reading. Like many other autistic adults, I have not been offered an assessment of needs or any support, even though this breaches statutory guidance and this has to change, services must be held to account, whether diagnoses are NHS or private.

Recognition of your difference and needs is your right and it is also the basis for what you can seek by way of support.

---

1 Aspies is a common term for people with Asperger's Syndrome in the autistic community.

2 This is a government strategy that was updated in April 2014 – it can be found at https://www.gov.uk/government/publications/think-autism-an-update-to-the-government-adult-autism-strategy.

Diagnosis late in life Hermione Heppel

"The more people I get to know, the more distinct and unique each person is"

I won't catalogue the bad memories; suffice it to say that they are no different from any other high-functioning autistic person's experience, where the impairment is not immediately obvious. It all came to a head three years ago, in my late fifties, when my boss told me that I have 'the kind of personality people avoid'. I resigned the following day, after eight years in a tech writer job that suited me perfectly, except for the fact that I made no real friends during that time.

As a child I seemed normal enough, if a bit precocious; I did well at school both in class and in sports and had no problems following instructions or picking up concepts, particularly in maths and science. All was well, except for one pattern that mystified me: I would frequently find myself confronted with defensiveness or hostility – or its close cousin, a careful little chat, like they are dealing with a wild animal – when I didn't think I'd said anything untoward. I became sensitised to this, but it still caught me unawares whenever it happened. I had no idea what I'd done or said wrong.

The only word I had to describe my unhappiness was 'depression'. Doctors, and I tried several during my university years, all sent me away with sugar pills so I tried therapy. To this day I believe they did more harm than good; they seemed to treat me with contempt, but they kept me on as a meal ticket. I think one of them thought I was a psychopath; when I finally found the courage to tell her I was leaving she actually uttered the phrase 'a danger to yourself and to others'.

But after my boss's comment I decided to try again. This time I went for CBT on the NHS. The main reason for choosing CBT was that it is bounded: the number of sessions is agreed in advance so there was no worry about extricating myself.

I requested a male therapist because I do seem to get on better with men, and I struck gold. I asked him to help me find out 'why people don't like me'. I watched him exercise his listening skills as I gave him my stream of consciousness. For once I didn't get the feeling of contempt that I'd had from the other therapists; I felt that he really was listening to me. On the third session I asked him whether he could give me some feedback now that he'd seen me twice, and he came back with the response: 'Have you heard of Asperger's?' Bingo. Six months later I had my assessment, and his insight was confirmed.

Suddenly there was an explanation for all the gaffes and misunderstandings, the awful things people have said to me over the years, the suspicion that I'm not a real person, that I'm spiritually disabled, born blind in the deepest possible way. All the unpleasantness could now be put down to something other than my moral character. I am not an evil person after all. The relief was palpable.

As it all sank in over the following months I realised that it also explained the 'physics, philosophy and floods of tears', the three degrees and no career, the spiritual search that underpins my life, the desperate, visceral need to figure out how the world works and to find a place in it where I would be accepted. Using the only tool at my disposal – logic – I had been struggling to understand what every spiritual tradition insists cannot be understood in this way. It's no wonder, looking back, that every non-judgmental inclusive 'safe to be yourself' group I tried to join soon found me too difficult to handle.

When I started meeting other Aspies I really did feel included, for the first time. We would share our experiences and all nod in recognition. I learned a great deal about how different Aspies are from one another, how we don't all conform to the stereotypes. We each seem to have a distinct pattern of intolerances, and it can be problematic when one's own intolerances clash with someone else's. Even so, there is a common underlying pattern which is hard to pin down and is not well encapsulated in the autism criteria. I gained considerable insight into how I appear to others, from meeting others like me. My own intolerance seems to be ambiguity. If something is not clear, I feel as if everything is going to fall apart.

Having the diagnosis so late in life means I have to separate the autism itself from the wounds that have been inflicted by people over the years – some well-meaning, some not – in response to the way my autism expresses itself. Feedback suggests that my body language (which includes my tone of voice and facial expression) doesn't match my words, so my words get misunderstood or lost in the noise. It is interesting that people who know me have a very different reaction to my writing from people I have never met. It seems a strange coincidence that of the three people I have met after they read my writing, two greeted me with the same words: 'I thought you would be bigger'. This was long before my diagnosis, but it suggests that I really do express myself much better in writing than in person. I'm taller than average, so it's logical to assume that they were not referring to my physical size.

I have learned over the years how to read people's body language, and at times I've demonstrated quite good insight into how individual people think and feel about themselves. My autism shows itself not to me, but to others. It would seem to be a blind spot in the way my own behaviour affects other people: I can see them, but I can't see myself from their point of view. I have very little idea just how big the blind spot is, because of course I can't see it.

What I do see are the hostile reactions and the unkind words, which make it very clear that I have got it wrong again. These are my wounds, and they have left me with a very thin skin and an ocean of bitter self-loathing just below the surface. This bitterness erupts unexpectedly far too often, even now – although with the new insight I am learning to control it. I have no right to expect others to tiptoe around my triggers like they're walking on eggshells. A surprising number of autistics I've read, and met, seem to have the idea that they are entitled to have all their 'needs met' by people who, after all, do have their own lives to lead, their own sore spots, distractions and gaps in awareness.

I spent many years going to Tai Chi classes, with the promise that they would help me to find a calm, peaceful space within myself. It had the opposite effect – I was dissolving into tears when everyone else was commenting how wonderful it was. In this case it was the other advanced students who pressed my trigger. One in particular would taunt me repeatedly, as a joke of course, about my 'busy little brain'. That fed right into the spiritual disability problem, and eventually I gave up Tai Chi, for ten years. I've now returned, with my new understanding of why I ask so many questions, and why I have a visceral need to know the answers; my teachers are sympathetic and for the first time I'm starting to 'get' the calming, meditation aspect of it, and to have patience with myself when I don't understand something. My Tai Chi is suddenly improving, including (to my astonishment) the partner work, which I thought I would never be able to do.

No, it's up to me to heal my own wounds, or at least manage them. The diagnosis doesn't let me off the hook. If I can't easily find the right words to say, why should I expect other people always to know how to deal compassionately with me? But the old habits, the bitterness, will take time to heal. I treasure the few friends I do have; I know they are genuine. Meanwhile I am learning to cope with ambiguity, at least where it doesn't really matter in a practical sense. Knowing that my difficulties have a biological basis makes them much easier to deal with.

I will always have to do my empathy the hard way, trying to remember not to project my own feelings, working from first principles, marshalling what I know about a person and trying to balance the fact that we are all the same with the fact that we are all different. Just because I'm different doesn't mean everyone else is the same, and just because someone appears to be relatively normal doesn't mean they have an easy life.

The more people I get to know, the more distinct and unique each person is, whether on the spectrum or not.

Since the diagnosis I've written two novels in a trilogy that I've called 'Poor in Spirit'. Or rather I should say they wrote themselves, in the space of about eight months. The first book, Flaming Sword, is now available on Amazon Kindle. Writing the books has helped me to clarify a lot of things in my mind, and in particular has helped with empathy tools because the story is, after all, about people and how they interact. In the third book, which has yet to be written, I shall discover through my characters whether I am in fact spiritually disabled and if so, I shall come to terms with it.

Meanwhile, I've given up on the spiritual and self-help groups altogether. Tai Chi is a martial art and I expect no more from it than that, and after finding solace in my new lathe I now exchange hints and tips on that vast and non-threatening subject at the local woodturning club.

I'm advised that it's a good idea to write a little explanation and carry it around in my wallet. There will be situations where it might help to pre-empt a lot of unpleasantness, for example when dealing with health professionals or the police. It doesn't need to be very long; something like 'Please don't take it personally if my behaviour seems odd; I am autistic and don't express myself very well in unfamiliar situations' will do. At the very least, it should start a conversation on the subject.

A journey of a self-identified professional autistic Lydia Andal

> **" I am much more confident and comfortable with identifying as autistic "**

I am a self-identified autistic.

I graduated with a 2:1 Degree in Business Management & Entrepreneurship and went on to work in the corporate field with roles as a Business Advisor and a Small Business Manager at a major bank before I went on to found my own Career Management Agency helping people advance in their career with Interview Coaching and CV preparation.

Since then I have worked with over 2,000 clients with many of those signing up for interview coaching often displaying autistic traits; they are very good at their job but struggle with navigating the unwritten rules of the interview process. They often say too little/too much or just say the 'wrong' thing and don't progress to the next stage of the recruitment process.

I found that I understood this group particularly well – it was like I could speak their language and help them 'open up' more and understand the rules in a way other people would struggle to do. I never realised I was autistic until many years later when I watched the 'Temple Grandin' HBO film.

Temple Grandin thinks in pictures – visual thinking is my way of thinking and I thought it was unique to me, but when I started researching autistic traits I realised I shared a lot of them. I then knew that the reason I always felt fundamentally different to everyone else around me at work and social events was because I was autistic.

I guessed this is also why I always connected well with those clients displaying 'autistic traits' in my career agency. I set up the agency because I was struggling in the corporate world. My work was always well-praised but I really struggled with the 'social networking' side of the workplace – I found it difficult to connect with other colleagues and managers at a social level because I didn't share their preference for 'superficial small talk' and my direct manner and preference for honesty meant I often found myself on the wrong side of 'office politics'.

Age 32 after much research I reluctantly accepted I was autistic. I say reluctantly because much of what is written about autism is quite negative and my positive autistic traits had no home in the clinical diagnosis process – so I didn't pursue it. Two years later I am much more confident and comfortable with identifying as autistic because I understand that I have key traits that make me good at my work; my attention to detail and ability to spot patterns in research and areas of interest lead to me identifying trends that others often miss. I also have hyper-focus and can work extremely quickly on a task when required.

I privately told my friends and sister that I was autistic and they were surprised although they commented that I did have 'specific traits' or 'ways of doing things' which now made more sense to them. I publicly told the world I was autistic in 'The autism issue' of a magazine I edited called *The New Idealist* and I have now published a book which explores the differences and pros/cons of self-diagnosis and clinical diagnosis.

I would like it if those involved in clinical diagnosis would refrain from discussing autism solely as an 'impairment' and instead recognise that autism is a spectrum with both challenges and strengths.

A personal journey Charles Burns

> **"Today I have accepted the condition, the depression has gone and only the empowerment remains"**

Our son was born on a cold February evening in 1991 and right from the start seemed subtly different in some vague, indefinable way. Our second child, he was the ideal baby, quiet and self-contained – except when hungry – with an enormous appetite. He adapted easily to our existing routine and then held us to it. Left alone in a cot he would lie awake and stare for hours, as though mesmerised, by the pattern on the inside of the hood. Always smiling, always happy and yet curiously quiet, living silently in a world of his own.

He was late doing everything. He walked at 18 months, uttered his first words at 2½ but couldn't speak a whole sentence until he was four. He's the only child I ever heard of who literally learned to use a computer before he learned to talk. He preferred playing on his own and would spend hours repeatedly driving toy cars in straight lines across the floor.

My partner became concerned and her concern increased as the years went by. Our son seemed to grow out of one obscure phase into another, each less normal than the last. Personally I found it hard to share this concern, my own parents kept saying: 'Oh don't worry, he's just like you were at that age, and you grew up OK!'

Our local Montessori nursery school couldn't teach him anything, although they did at least keep him (in the 1960s I was expelled from a London nursery school after refusing to take part and just sitting at the side of the room). His primary school years were worse: in year two he was placed on the special-needs register as he couldn't – seemed like wouldn't – concentrate on or finish any of his work. He was frequently left alone in the reading corner, reading and re-reading books until he exhausted their library. To me it just seemed as though he was teaching himself to speak by reading; a sensible thing to do and pretty much what I did at his age.

My partner began to read about Asperger's Syndrome. In the mid-to-late 1990s it was a little-known condition. Trawling the internet she found a lot of information and presented it to me one evening, suggesting the description fitted our son very well and that perhaps we should seek a diagnosis for him. As I read it I experienced a shock of recognition which I'll never forget and then the doors seemed to slam shut in my mind. I rejected it utterly.

'This isn't him' I said. 'Our son doesn't have this kind of problem at all.'

The awful truth was that it wasn't my son I was reading about, but me! What followed were some of the worst years of our lives. That our marriage survived at all is testimony to my partner's tolerance and stamina. She went ahead and sought a diagnosis for our son, a process which turned out to be long and painful. She did this with no support from me and in the teeth of opposition from our son's primary school, who insisted that such things are best left to professionals. Sadly, she fought this battle on her own.

Gradually it became clear even to me that the school was letting him down completely. He became increasingly unhappy and his elder sister reported to us the teasing he was being subjected to on a daily basis. In denial as I was, even I could see the necessity of moving him. At the end of Year 3 we transferred him to a Steiner school, which turned out to be far better suited to his temperament.

This was followed in Year 4 by medical diagnosis that our son had Asperger's Syndrome. The whole subject of autism became a kind of a minefield in our marriage; we simply couldn't enter it without verbal explosions. Gradually it seemed as though arguments were all that was left of our relationship. I was caught in turmoil, recognising more and more the parallels between our son's problems and my own

childhood, and yet unable to talk about this to anybody, least of all my partner. Eventually, at my suggestion, we sought help from Relate in an effort to keep the family together.

They didn't help. Our counsellor was of the opinion that the only way she could really help was by helping us to separate, which I refused to contemplate. However she also expressed the view that I should seek psychiatric help, as I seemed to lack any empathy for my partner's point of view. Spurred on by imminent separation I did seek such help, approaching my GP for a referral. There at last I was able to talk of my fears regarding Asperger's Syndrome and was referred to a specialist in autism. My own diagnosis, carried out privately, was swift and sure.

According to the autism specialist, whom I met in 2001, I presented as a classic case of undiagnosed Asperger's Syndrome.

Gradually questions began to sort themselves out in my head. How could such a thing be possible? How can one live all one's life with such a condition and not know it? Yet slowly I realised that I always did know; as soon as I heard about the condition I recognised it. All my life I have regarded myself as being oddly different – somehow an island – set apart from other people.

Diagnosis was an extraordinary experience. The specialist was most interested in my past; she asked about my entire childhood – from my expulsion from nursery school to my time at primary school – and in particular about my friendless adolescent years at boarding school in the 1970s. Without going into all the details the process brought out many further parallels between my son and myself which hadn't occurred even to me.

We explored my life-long interest in art and drawing, as well as my current obsession with the very particular art of silhouette cutting – which has become my profession. It was explained to me that people with Asperger's Syndrome often excel in such obscure fields, precisely because of their ability, or need, to shut themselves off from the world and concentrate fully on their chosen subject.

We also explored my years at art college, in the early 1980s, when I first discovered Shintaido. My partner and I met at art college. Coming to England from Japan she brought with her an extraordinary avant-garde martial art called Shintaido, which she set up as a student-union club and began to teach. I was so taken by it that I fell in love with both the art and the teacher; both have been the mainstays of my life ever since! I remember my art-student days as a wonderful time, when I finally seemed to 'come out of my shell' and start to make friends with those around me. I lost much of the physical clumsiness and social awkwardness which had so dogged my childhood. I began to enjoy myself: both my art and a new feeling of 'being me'.

The specialist found all this very significant. She explained to me that young people with Asperger's Syndrome benefit from an intensive combination of artistic and physical, movement-based therapies. She couldn't really imagine a more appropriate life for me than a full-time fine-art education combined with the Shintaido I was practising in the evenings. She felt that I had done very well in finding my own way to cope with my autistic problems, that my discovery of Shintaido was a happy accident and that I had somehow self-therapied myself out of the worst aspects of my condition.

Looking back at those years this does make sense. My big problem was always communication, both with others and with myself (e.g. in putting names to my own feelings). In Shintaido I found kumite (a partner practice aimed at improving non-verbal communication with others) and meditation (a kind of communication with oneself). I also found eiko: a noisy, free, cathartic movement – unique to Shintaido – which works wonders for self confidence. Then there's a whole range of movements loosely called hikari, which tie everything together and foster an intuitive understanding of the subtle ways we all influence each other. Lastly there are the kata: formal sequences of movement through which I have learned to control my body, improve my posture and lose forever the awkward 'way of moving' of my childhood (for which I was so teased at school). Through a combination of all these things I have found my own voice as well as the confidence and means to express it. But it did take time.

After leaving art college in 1984, with a first-class degree in Fine Art, I was faced with a dilemma. I was aware I had changed a lot yet was terrified at the thought of seeking employment. To me it seemed as though this would be like going back to school, back to an environment where people would try to control who I was and try to make me 'fit in'. I knew my communication skills were poor and had no confidence that I could cope with the office politics of a workplace environment. Lacking a diagnosis I had no words to express this so described myself as one of nature's natural self-employed: a kind of island in the sea of work.

In 1985 I began to make ends meets by taking a weekend pitch as a street artist at Covent Garden in London, drawing pencil portraits of tourists and other passers-by for £5 a go. I was very good at it! I remained there for over ten years, during which time I got married, fathered two children and bought a house. By 1995 the price had risen to £15 and I had started to cut silhouette profiles as a sideline. Very slowly – throughout that decade – my communication skills improved. The combination of on-going Shintaido practice and having to speak to the public in Covent Garden began to have an effect. To my great surprise, in the mid 1990s, people began to book me as an 'artist-entertainer' to cut silhouettes of their guests at parties and corporate events. As a young man I had always hated parties and would have run a mile to avoid such employment.

Today I work full time in the events and entertainment industry, and spend my life travelling the country (and occasionally abroad) from one event to another cutting silhouettes with scissors. This obscure eighteenth-century art has become my livelihood. I have been booked for some extraordinary events and met, and cut portraits of, many famous people. I have written a book about silhouettes and even made a documentary film.

Many years have now passed since my diagnosis in 2001. At first I alternated between periods of deep depression – realising autism was something I could never be cured of – and periods of real empowerment. The empowerment came from a feeling that I had been given the knowledge I needed to cope even better than I already was. Both of these are true. Today I have accepted the condition, the depression has gone and only the empowerment remains. Soon after my diagnosis I qualified as a Shintaido instructor and have taught a regular weekly class for a number of years. I have also presented Shintaido exercise at autism conferences, including Autscape.

My partner and I are still together and arguments between us are largely a thing of the past. Our son left the Steiner school and went on to secondary education with the support of a specialist ASD unit in a mainstream school, followed by sixth-form studies at a private school. He recently completed a degree course in Japanese studies at Manchester University which, among other achievements, has involved him living independently in Japan for a year. He has now entered the world of work (which I found so impossible at his age) by taking a job as an in-house translator for a Japanese software company.

The ground under my feet Joe

" I thought that was odd because I didn't see myself as suffering, just different "

I was diagnosed with Asperger's Syndrome in May 1995 at the age of 11. Apparently it was a major struggle for my parents to get a diagnosis. I was probably lucky to have a diagnosis when young, but in the years after being diagnosed the impact it had was mostly negative.

It's hard to tell whether the changes that followed were due to my diagnosis, or because I was going through adolescence, or because I was bullied a lot worse than I was before. I also realised I was gay at that age. Because all this happened in a short space of time, it's hard to pinpoint what influenced the changes in me.

In primary school before I was diagnosed, I was certainly very different from others. I used to skip up and down in the same area of the playground every day. I'd do this in a very repetitive way, and make up stories while doing so to tell anybody who would listen. I had many obsessive interests, including geography (I memorised all the capitals of all the countries in the world) and politics. I'd get very worried and concerned about events that were going on, and very driven to make the world around me a better place. I once wrote a letter to Terry Waite after he had been released from captivity, and to John

Major suggesting a solution to the Northern Ireland crisis.
My parents talked me out of sending the second letter for fear
of being targeted by MI5. I used to stay behind after school to
clean up the classroom, and once spent all the pocket money
I saved up getting an expensive toy for my younger brother.
I could be badly behaved too though. I remember being yelled
at by my Dad a lot for doing something naughty during those
years.

I realised I was different from other people before I was diagnosed, but I didn't see it as a bad thing. I had very bad hand-
writing and wasn't good at P.E., but I also had an excellent
memory, a vivid imagination and got good marks in school.
I was eccentric, but compassionate. I did get bullied, and
although it wasn't nice it didn't really affect me at a core level
and I didn't change my behaviour because of it. I didn't have
any friends my age, but that didn't matter as I preferred talking to adults anyway. I had less self-censorship than even
people my age at the time; I'd cry easily and say whatever
came into my head. These traits would look strange to the
outside observer, but I think they were fundamentally
harmless.

When I was diagnosed, I initially didn't see it as a big deal as
I didn't see myself as sick or disabled. I remember being puz-
zled when I saw something being written about Asperger's
sufferers. I thought that was odd because I didn't see myself
as suffering, just different. I think that my parents reacted
more strongly to the diagnosis though, my Dad yelled at me
less, and they both became a lot more protective, almost to
the point of helicoptering. When I started secondary school

in September 1995, it was assumed that I would get bullied from the first day. I had a special needs teacher shadowing me at break times, and my Dad would walk with me to and from school. Although there was an atmosphere of trepidation at the time, I didn't act or feel any differently than I did before I was diagnosed.

The real watershed occurred in February 1996 when I was taken to see a specialist in Asperger's Syndrome. I thought it would be like many other visits to specialists, where I and my mother would talk about my quirks and we'd all agree that I was a little bit odd but also very intelligent and basically OK This meeting was different. She was very well spoken, and exuded authority. We spoke about my habit of skipping up and down in certain areas in a rigid way. She referred to it as 'jumping, flapping and making noises', and told me I had to stop it right away. My other quirks were mentioned, and although she wasn't as disapproving of them, she noted them in same style that a doctor would note the symptoms of a disease.

I never skipped again in school after that meeting, and gradually stopped doing it at home over the course of a few weeks. This might not seem like something major to the outside observer, but it wrecked my self-esteem virtually overnight. While it did look strange to the outside, that habit was something that my whole identity hung on. While doing this, I could make up stories, make sense of the world and let off excess energy. It was tolerated by my parents and teachers so I never saw the harm in it. Moving about in a pre-defined pattern is such a core part of my identity that even when I suppressed it, it would pop up again in less obvious ways.

Later on in school I used to walk around certain corridors during break times, and later I would walk around certain streets in my hometown in the same way. In adult life, I travelled on the entire railway networks of several countries. I used to be ashamed of this, but now I'm realising that it's such a core part of me that needs to be incorporated into any lifestyle that I have.

I started reading more about Asperger's Syndrome, but it was extremely depressing reading about the life stories of people with this condition. It seemed that my life would involve being bullied throughout school, and in my adult life I would be impoverished and lonely and struggle to exist. I read about famous people in history who may have had Asperger's Syndrome, like Einstein, or Newton or Thomas Jefferson. But that never convinced me very much as I remember undergoing five hours of constant tests with modern equipment to be diagnosed which you couldn't give to people in the past. I thought it was telling that there was no-one in modern times who did well in life and was undeniably diagnosed with Asperger's. It was a quite a shock going from seeing myself as someone who was intelligent and creative and would do well in life to someone who was disabled and inadequate, and would live a limited life on the margins of society.

After that meeting, I became ashamed of the quirks and traits that I had and began to suppress or hide them. I pretended I didn't know any more than other peers did, and started a new obsession with trying to fit in with my peers and be normal. I rejected all special needs help that the school had offered, and walked home by myself. I think rejecting help and trying to achieve things by myself was a positive step, but trying to fit in was not. Starting from the Autumn of 1996, I was bullied more intensely than previously and this remained constant for most of my school career.

The change was that unlike before, I took on board the insults that people made. Perhaps the more intense bullying would have happened anyway, or perhaps they sensed insecurity in me that wasn't there before. I think that the difference between pre and post diagnosis was that previously when people bullied me, I saw it as their problem because they were being stupid and immature, whereas after I was diagnosed, I saw myself as the defective one, who had to live up to their standard. There was one other boy in my class who reminded me of what I used to be, so I bullied him in order to deflect attention from me and to secure my place in the class hierarchy. I now realise that I was projecting my own self-hatred on to him. I hope he's turned out OK.

After the meeting, I felt an anger that wasn't there before. It was inarticulate at first, but over the next two years this feeling was put into words. I didn't feel like I was sick in the same way that somebody with a physical illness, or a mental illness, was. I felt that someone from on high had decreed that I was ill, and that in order to be 'cured' I would have to suppress core parts of my identity, and abase myself in front of people who aren't ill...and get rejected anyway. It seemed to me that a lot of the 'treatment' for Asperger's Syndrome was to make the person with Asperger's less 'offensive' to wider society, even if this is at the expense of the well-being of the person with Asperger's.

At the age of 14, I got sick of trying to fit in, and rebelled against my peers. I deliberately behaved in a weird and obnoxious way, and attacked and tried to bury my previous false self with the same ferocity I used to attack and bury the person I was pre-diagnosis. I was still bullied, but occasionally I was able to talk back and sometimes fight back. Some parts of myself pre-diagnosis I brought back to the surface, like my memory for many facts, and desire to learn, but other parts of my identity I kept suppressed because I felt they made me vulnerable.

My compassion for other people was one of the traits I felt made me vulnerable, so I tried to suppress that emotion and be as difficult and obnoxious as possible.

The Asperger's specialist didn't disappear from my life after that meeting in 1996. I was invited to take part in a social skills study/class for teenagers with Asperger's Syndrome. Every few months or so I would go to a class in London, where we would talk to each other and do certain exercises. It was a nice respite from school, but I don't think I gained a massive amount from it. She told my Mum I 'only had a brush of Asperger' (which made me wonder if I had been mis-diagnosed), and to me 'Don't let the autism beat you' (which reinforced the drive to suppress who I was). Most of the time she was polite to people in the group, but occasionally she used the same technique on other people that she used on me. I remember distinctly when a kid in the group was flapping his hands when talking. She interrupted him, pointed out he was flapping his hands, and said that 'Perhaps the reason why you don't have many friends is because you do things like this'. I hope he didn't take what she said on-board.

Despite this, I wouldn't call her a bad person or even unethical and sloppy in her work. She helped my parents to get the right kind of support for me, and intervened to stop me from getting expelled after I got into a fight with another pupil at school where he came off worse. She has helped set up one of the first publications of autistic self-advocacy in the UK. Research into Asperger's Syndrome was still in its early days in the mid 1990s and like all scientists, she was fumbling around in the dark.

I met her several more times up until my early 20s, and after seeing the way she interacts with others, and reflecting on the interactions she made with myself and other people, I am almost certain that she is on the autistic spectrum herself. I spoke about it with my parents and they told me that they had come to that conclusion as well. Obviously the past can't be changed, but I do wonder if she had said to me something on the lines of 'Look, life will be difficult for you, but you can still have Asperger's Syndrome and do well in life and I am an example of this. But you need to make some compromises with the outside world', then perhaps my experience after diagnosis would have been less traumatic.

From my teens to my early 20s, I alternated between being angry towards wider society, and trying (and occasionally suc-ceeding) to fit in – between despairing and being angry in a constructive way. However, my life has been richer and more fulfilling than I expected it to be in my teens, and this has boosted my self-confidence. I've realised that my pre-diagnosis self is buried rather than broken. However, to an extent, it still needs to be buried in order to cope with the outside world.

My social skills have improved over time, and when communicating with people I try to avoid behaviours that cause harm. From a medical point of view, my condition has greatly improved as I am more able to socialise with other people than in the past. However, my definition of being cured would be to regain the self-assurance and self-confidence that I had before I was diagnosed, in a world where autistic traits that don't cause harm to you and/or others are accepted.

Calm, almost too calm Panda Mery

"The diagnosis also helped me to reinterpret some traumatic experiences"

My understanding of how autism is an integral part of myself has been a long journey. I have always been different, eccentric, with very few friends. In primary school I was nicknamed 'dictionary' and in secondary school was bullied. I identified as a techie person and spent a lot of time with computers and online. Around 1998, when I was in my thirties, I read a review of the book Shadow Syndromes, which made me wonder whether I might be autistic.

The review picked among other things on the incapacity of one 'patient' to 'clap in time to music'. This, in particular, resonated strongly with me. I can only clap in rhythm by visually syncing with another person's clapping. I had never met or read of anyone with the same difficulty for what is apparently such a simple task. (It is ironic that this is not considered a characteristic autistic symptom.)

Reading more about autism and doing some online tests convinced me I was autistic and I self-diagnosed as having Asperger's Syndrome. However coming from a medical family I was very aware of the unreliability of self-diagnoses generally and my family did not agree with this self-diagnosis. Tests, especially online ones, didn't seem to be much more reliable. This resulted in believing that I was likely autistic, as many of my behaviours and past experiences matched some I had read about as being autistic, but not in the confidence to identify as autistic.

In 2013, in my late forties, I eventually sought a professional diagnosis. The reasons were two-fold.

Having previously worked as a software developer, a technologist and a journalist, I was unemployed, doing voluntary work and had decided to go back to university to do an MA. I thought a diagnosis could help me (as I eventually dropped out, this outcome was not fulfilled).

Also I had been wrongfully arrested. When I attempted to take the tube at Southwark station on 2005-07-28, police officers found my behaviour suspicious and decided to stop and search and subsequently arrest me as a potential terrorist. I thought a diagnosis would help if I was arrested again (this has not happened so far).

To get the diagnosis I went to my GP equipped with a printout of the information page for GPs from the National Autistic Society (NAS) and asked to be referred. My GP did not know anything about autism and asked me for a list of symptoms on one side of an A4 page and for a blood test. I attempted to explain that a blood test was irrelevant (and that I have an aversion to needles) but as I wanted the referral I went along with this request. (This GP also made some derogatory comments about my autism to my wife and we have both since changed surgery.)

In May 2013, a neuropsychologist eventually diagnosed that from information I had given him 'there are features in social interaction and communication that, in the absence of other diagnoses, places you on the autistic spectrum – of the Asperger's type.'

The validation from this diagnosis had the effect of enabling me to identify as autistic and to start to explore my autistic identity. Only after this professional diagnosis did I feel a sense of belonging, the confidence to join groups such as the Asperger London Area Group (ALAG) and to attend the Autscape conference; whereas before I felt I was not entitled to do so.

The diagnosis also helped me to reinterpret some traumatic experiences. It has made me realise that when police officers had found my behaviour suspicious, it was because of how they had interpreted some of my typical autistic behaviour, such as a lack of eye contact with them (i.e., I was 'avoiding them') and how I was dealing with the sensory-rich environment of the tube station. When I was made to wait in the entrance of the station before being led to a police van, some station's alarms were ringing; I am hypersensitive to sound, but as my hands were still handcuffed I could not block my ears. When I was eventually processed, the custody sergeant found me 'calm on arrival [at the police station], almost too calm' and as a consequence I was 'placed in a video cell on half hourly checks'. Again, my behaviour was found to be atypical.

During the police interview, some questions about my laptop, such as 'has it got anything on there about plans for any terrorism act?' and 'has it got anything on there that might be

construed as causing a public nuisance?', particularly both-
ered me. The correct answers would have been 'yes' as I have
a word processor, an email client, etc. that could all be useful
to a terrorist and most likely can be construed to be of use
for anything including causing a public nuisance, however, I
realised that such answers would not have been been helpful
to me and challenged the questions when the investigating
officer just wanted answers.

Since the arrest I have become alcohol and fructose intolerant
and I suspect this was a reaction to the stress. Policing in
London and what happens to innocent individuals when they
encounter the police became one of my special interests and I
have researched, written and campaigned on civil and human
rights issues such as the National DNA Database and the stop
and search powers.

A year after my diagnosis, I publicly 'outed' myself and started some autism activism: I sent a contribution to a Home Affairs Committee inquiry into policing and mental health calling for police officers to realise that an atypical behaviour can be just different rather than suspicious; to consider hyper- and hypo-sensitivities that individuals may have; and to use clearer interviewing questions.

I am glad I sought out a diagnosis as it has been very helpful, but paradoxically this journey has helped me realise that for what is a neurodivergence,[1] we should not need a medical validation. The medical pathway is not the best one, what we need is more legitimisation of self-diagnoses and acceptance of neurodiversity.

---

1 See Panda's piece on terminology for further explanation of this term.

A spiritual shift Jan Brooking

"I have been more relaxed, joyous and interesting to be with"

'All these years we thought you were you and now you're telling us you're someone else!'

Consternation and disbelief, coupled with a sense of having been betrayed or 'duped', may be among the most disconcerting reactions to your disclosure of your diagnosis. However, with time these will abate and I have noticed, much to my interest and relief, that those who were initially so ardently opposed to my news, have now become my most understanding and compassionate advocates and champions. A diagnosis of autism or Asperger's will not only challenge you but also those closest to you and become a growing point for all concerned!

'Everyone has Asperger's these days. It's the latest thing!' retorted one friend, wounding me to the core.

If you only knew the pain and anxiety it has caused in my life, I thought, vowing never to mention the A word again. But, one year on, here we were calmly and quietly sharing our impressions of this way of being in the world with healing occurring on both sides.

Receiving my diagnosis has given me an inner assuredness and a confidence that is slowly and steadily growing. I tend

now to have more patience with myself when things are difficult and have found two ways to enjoy my Aspie qualities.

Firstly, I frequently utilize my Asperger's humour to bring
levity into people's lives. A sense of the ridiculous and an
alternate reality never goes amiss! Secondly, my passion for
spiritual work and an abiding interest in intercessory prayer
provide me with a purpose in the world. My world is regularly
filled with people who come to share my meditative space
which I have now been freed to construct through my acceptance of my eccentricities.

One of my closest friends remarked that since accepting my
diagnosis of Asperger's, I have been more relaxed, joyous and
interesting to be with.

So, to anyone who has just discovered that they are on the
spectrum, take heart and know that during the darkest
moments there are gifts waiting to be unveiled and that the
struggle for self knowledge and an understanding of our place
in the scheme of things, is a creative force that can serve and
enrich us all.

Terminology Panda Mery

I am not a person with autism. I am an autistic person.

Receiving a diagnosis or identifying as autistic – can be very empowering and often entails talking and/or writing about autism. There are many words and expressions to choose from. You might have noticed that the contributors to this booklet express different preferences in their writing. To help you navigate your way through this terminology, here are a few of my choices and their implications.

You can choose whether to use identity-first (I am an autistic person) or person-first (I am a person with autism) language. As autism is an integral part of who we are – the way our brains and bodies work – many autistics are keen on the use of identity-first language and refer to themselves as 'autistics'. I find person-first language (being called 'a person with autism') offensive as it implies that we should strive for a state when we are 'without autism'. A useful way to think about this is that you would say a person with a cold, but not some-one with Jewishness, or with left-handedness. Of course I also respect each individual's choice of the language they use to refer to themselves.

This distinction is linked to how you consider our differences and how we fit in society. I know of two basic models. The medical model, the most common in our society, explains the difficulties we may have as caused by us not fitting in. To improve our lives, we must change (e.g., forcing ourselves to look others in the eyes, not stimming,[1] etc.). The social model, which I and many other autistics prefer, considers that if someone has difficulties fitting in that is because there are barriers that should be removed; society must work to eliminate discrimination and accept us as we are in all our diversity. While the medical model finds autism to be a problem that must ideally be cured and suggests interventions, the social model promotes equality, respect and inclusion.

Autism Spectrum Disorder (ASD), on the spectrum, Asperger's Syndrome or type, Aspie, high (HFA) and low functioning and classic autism, etc. – a great many terms are used to label us, but we tend to use fewer to express our identities. One reason for so many is to reflect the diversity of autistics. A common saying, attributed to Lorna Wing, is that once you've met one autistic, you've met one autistic. Several of these words classify us along a spectrum with abilities ranging from very poor (low-functioning autism and classic autism) to above average (high-functioning autism and Asperger). This neat continuum, however, does not match the more complex reality. Some autistics will find some tasks very easy some days and impossible to do at other times; individual profiles tend to be spiky and changeable. Although my diagnosis was 'on the autistic spectrum – of the Asperger's type', I feel that it is more inclusive to identify simply as autistic and support everyone in this constellation of diagnoses and identities.

What about everyone else – the non-autistics? A word often used by autistics (and others) to describe most of those who are not is 'neurotypical' (i.e., have a typical brain), abbreviated as NT. The world is made up of neurodiverse individuals:

people with a variety of brains and minds, most are neuro-typical and some are neurodivergent including autistics and everyone else whose brain is not typical (e.g., epileptic, dys-lexic, etc.). Being neurodivergent is not intrinsically positive or negative. The social model celebrates a neurodiverse world in which autistics are fully accepted with all our differences, a world I want to live in.

To explore some of these issues in more depth, here are a few good starting points:

www.larry-arnold.net/Autonomy/index.php/autonomy/article/view/OP1/html_1

www.autisticadvocacy.org/identity-first-language/

www.neurocosmopolitanism.com/neurodiversity-some-basic-terms-definitions/

---

1 'Stimming' is self stimulatory behaviour such as hand flapping or spinning.

Contributor biographies

Alison

Alison is an Asperger's mum to two autistic girls, working from home supporting her husband's business. She first heard of Asperger's seven years ago, researching causes of her eldest daughter's behaviour. She was diagnosed two years ago. Her journey led her into 'quiet background campaigning and advocacy'. Website: evolutian.wix.com/planetautism Facebook: www.facebook.com/PlanetOughtism Twitter: www.twitter.com/Planet_Autism 'I don't much chat – I inform!'

Anne Moxom (illustrator)

Anne is a designer and illustrator, living with her family in the New Forest. She has three boys who have diagnoses of autism, dyspraxia and ADD. She also received an autism spectrum diagnosis in her early 40s. In between a busy family life, Anne dabbles: writing, illustrating, jewellery designing and volunteering for a charity supporting families with additional needs. The support of her friends and family and getting out into the forest with the boys keep her sane.

Caroline Hearst (editor)

Caroline is a late diagnosed autistic adult. She is the founder and a director of AutAngel, www.autangel.org.uk, and runs Autism Matters, www.autismmatters.org.uk, which offers autism awareness training and consultancy. She has two sons one of whom is autistic and both of whom currently live in New Zealand. She manages more work on her allotment in theory than in practice, concocts a soup now and then and occasionally creates photo collages.

Charles Burns

Charles is a married father of two, who became aware of his autism because of his son's diagnosis. He is a self-employed artist entertainer who cuts silhouettes in record time, details at www.roving-artist.com, and is also a Shintaido instructor, see www.shintaido.co.uk

Panda Mery

Panda is married and lives in London. He started fully accepting his autism when 47 years old. He is a team member of AutAngel, volunteering with the Restart Project and as an Independent Custody Visitor, involved in research and maintaining a calendar of autism-related events. His website is at gizmonaut.net

Jan Brooking

Jan lives in Christchurch New Zealand and has a background in special education, fostering, and pastoral care. In 2010 she co-founded Aspiehelp a peer support service offering information, advocacy, mentoring, peer support, counselling, workplace training & monitoring, social events, and practical assistance. In 2014 she received an award from Autism New Zealand in conjunction with the Ministry of Health for outstanding achievement and work in the community.

Joe

Joe lives in the UK and works as a CCTV operator. His obsessions include: travelling, making railway maps, collecting rocks and arguing about politics and autism rights on the internet. He might found a new nation state later this year!

Hermione Heppel (pseudonym)

Hermione has been married for 30 years, and has two sons in their late twenties. Her woodworking hobby occasionally brings in commissions, and she also enjoys scuba diving and growing vegetables. Her pet vices are red wine, Sudoku and organising things with little success. There is information about her books, and a blog, on www.zendao.net

Laura Williams

Laura is 33 years old and lives in Surrey with her cat Mitzi. She is studying for a BSc in Animal Behaviour, and works at a cat rescue centre. She was diagnosed with Asperger's at the age of 25, having suspected for a few years before that.

Liane Collins

Liane lives in Worcester now but is from north-east England. She has been married for 25 years and has an adult son with autism. She is a counsellor and tutor in private practice specialising in issues related to ASCs and working online. Website and blogs can be found at www.silverleafcounselling.co.uk. She is also a mad cat lady!

Lydia Andal

Lydia is 34, lives in Manchester, runs a career management agency and is the author of *Am I autistic? A guide to autism & Asperger's self-diagnosis for adults* (published by New Idealist Limited, 2015). Lydia also edited *The New Idealist* magazine: 'The autism issue' is available for free download at www.amiautistic.com

Resources Caroline Hearst

There has been an explosion of autism related activity on the internet in recent years. There are many lists, forums, Facebook groups, blogs, etc. If you spend time in cyberspace it is worth checking out some of these and seeing what suits you. AutAngel's suggestions are on our resources page at www.autangel.org.uk/resources.html.

If you want to meet other autistic people in real life the picture is more varied; some areas have active support groups, while others have nothing, or groups run by professionals whose agenda does not always work for us. I heartily recommend Autscape though – this is an annual conference/retreat run by and for autistic people (although non-autistics are welcome too). Details are at www.autscape.org.

There are also a plethora of books about autism. For women I highly recommend the seminal publication Jean Kearns Miller (Ed). *Women from another planet?: Our lives in the universe of autism*. There are many more books listed on AutAngel's resource page. Despite the fact that the diagnostic term Asperger's Syndrome has gone from the DSM diagnostic manual it is still often used to describe some autistic people. *The complete guide to Asperger's Syndrome* by Tony Attwood gives a good overview of autisms that might not be identified until later in life.

Enjoy exploring all the information out there about autism, there are plenty of different approaches, so it is worth checking out various authors and finding those whose approach resonates with your values and outlook.

Acknowledgements

AutAngel would like to thank:

The National Lottery for funding this reprint through their National Lottery Community Fund.

Anne Moxom for generously creating illustrations especially for us and graciously accommodating quirky requests.

Cameron Armstrong and Edward Crane, students in the Department of Typography & Graphic Communication at the University of Reading, for their creative and consultative graphic design.

Ruth Goodwin for unstinting support cheerfully offered regardless of unsocial hours and unrealistic timeframes.

Viv Mitchell for proof-reading and helping with copy editing despite relentless changes.

Last but definitely not least all the contributors for making this booklet possible by sharing their stories.